I0691158

My Ultimate Weight Loss Planner FITNESS JOURNAL YEAR

Activinotes

Activinotes

DAILY JOURNALS, PLANNERS, NOTEBOOKS AND OTHER BLANK BOOKS

All Rights reserved. No part of this book may be reproduced or used in any way or form or by any means whether electronic or mechanical, this means that you cannot record or photocopy any material ideas or tips that are provided in this book.

Copyright 2016

DAY: _____

NAME: _____

	DESCRIPTION	QTY	PROTEINS	VEGGIES	FRUITS & NUTS	FATS
BREAKFAST **TIME**						
TOTAL						

LUNCH **TIME**						
TOTAL						

DINNER **TIME**						
TOTAL						

SNACKS **TIME**	

	CORE BODY	UPPER BODY	LOWER BODY
EXERCISES			
SETS			
REPS			
WEIGHTS			
REST TIME			

	WARM UP	COOL DOWN
ACTIVITY		
SETS		
REPS		
TIME		
DIST		
INTENSITY		

GOALS: _____

_____

_____

_____

_____

_____

_____

_____

_____

DAY: _____

NAME: _____

	DESCRIPTION	QTY	PROTEINS	VEGGIES	FRUITS & NUTS	FATS
BREAKFAST						
TIME						
TOTAL						

LUNCH						
TIME						
TOTAL						

DINNER						
TIME						
TOTAL						

SNACKS	
TIME	

	CORE BODY	UPPER BODY	LOWER BODY
EXERCISES			
SETS			
REPS			
WEIGHTS			
REST TIME			

	WARM UP	COOL DOWN
ACTIVITY		
SETS		
REPS		
TIME		
DIST		
INTENSITY		

GOALS: _____

_____

_____

_____

_____

_____

_____

_____

DAY: _____

NAME: _____

	DESCRIPTION	QTY	PROTEINS	VEGGIES	FRUITS & NUTS	FATS
BREAKFAST TIME ☐						
TOTAL						

LUNCH TIME ☐						
TOTAL						

DINNER TIME ☐						
TOTAL						

SNACKS TIME ☐	

	CORE BODY	UPPER BODY	LOWER BODY
EXERCISES			
SETS			
REPS			
WEIGHTS			
REST TIME			

	WARM UP	COOL DOWN
ACTIVITY		
SETS		
REPS		
TIME		
DIST		
INTENSITY		

GOALS: _____

_____

_____

_____

_____

_____

_____

_____

_____

_____

DAY: _____

NAME: _____

	DESCRIPTION	QTY	PROTEINS	VEGGIES	FRUITS & NUTS	FATS
BREAKFAST						
TIME						
TOTAL						

LUNCH						
TIME						
TOTAL						

DINNER						
TIME						
TOTAL						

SNACKS	
TIME	

	CORE BODY	UPPER BODY	LOWER BODY
EXERCISES			
SETS			
REPS			
WEIGHTS			
REST TIME			

	WARM UP	COOL DOWN
ACTIVITY		
SETS		
REPS		
TIME		
DIST		
INTENSITY		

GOALS: _____

_____

_____

_____

_____

_____

_____

_____

DAY: _____

NAME: _____

		DESCRIPTION	QTY	PROTEINS	VEGGIES	FRUITS & NUTS	FATS
BREAKFAST							
TIME							
TOTAL							

		DESCRIPTION	QTY	PROTEINS	VEGGIES	FRUITS & NUTS	FATS
LUNCH							
TIME							
TOTAL							

		DESCRIPTION	QTY	PROTEINS	VEGGIES	FRUITS & NUTS	FATS
DINNER							
TIME							
TOTAL							

SNACKS	
TIME	

	CORE BODY	UPPER BODY	LOWER BODY
EXERCISES			
SETS			
REPS			
WEIGHTS			
REST TIME			

	WARM UP	COOL DOWN
ACTIVITY		
SETS		
REPS		
TIME		
DIST		
INTENSITY		

GOALS: _____

_____

_____

_____

_____

_____

_____

_____

_____

DAY: _____

NAME: _____

	DESCRIPTION	QTY	PROTEINS	VEGGIES	FRUITS & NUTS	FATS
BREAKFAST						
TIME						
TOTAL						

LUNCH						
TIME						
TOTAL						

DINNER						
TIME						
TOTAL						

SNACKS	
TIME	

	CORE BODY	UPPER BODY	LOWER BODY
EXERCISES			
SETS			
REPS			
WEIGHTS			
REST TIME			

	WARM UP	COOL DOWN
ACTIVITY		
SETS		
REPS		
TIME		
DIST		
INTENSITY		

GOALS: _____

_____

_____

_____

_____

_____

_____

_____

_____

DAY: _____

NAME: _____

		DESCRIPTION	QTY	PROTEINS	VEGGIES	FRUITS & NUTS	FATS
BREAKFAST							
TIME							
TOTAL							

LUNCH							
TIME							
TOTAL							

DINNER							
TIME							
TOTAL							

SNACKS	
TIME	

	CORE BODY	UPPER BODY	LOWER BODY
EXERCISES			
SETS			
REPS			
WEIGHTS			
REST TIME			

	WARM UP	COOL DOWN
ACTIVITY		
SETS		
REPS		
TIME		
DIST		
INTENSITY		

GOALS: _____

_____

_____

_____

_____

_____

_____

_____

_____

DAY: _____

NAME: _____

	DESCRIPTION	QTY	PROTEINS	VEGGIES	FRUITS & NUTS	FATS
BREAKFAST						
TIME						
▢						
TOTAL						

LUNCH						
TIME						
▢						
TOTAL						

DINNER						
TIME						
▢						
TOTAL						

SNACKS	
TIME	
▢	

	CORE BODY	UPPER BODY	LOWER BODY
EXERCISES			
SETS			
REPS			
WEIGHTS			
REST TIME			

	WARM UP	COOL DOWN
ACTIVITY		
SETS		
REPS		
TIME		
DIST		
INTENSITY		

GOALS: _____

_____

_____

_____

_____

_____

_____

_____

DAY: _____

NAME: _____

		DESCRIPTION	QTY	PROTEINS	VEGGIES	FRUITS & NUTS	FATS
BREAKFAST							
TIME							
TOTAL							

LUNCH							
TIME							
TOTAL							

DINNER							
TIME							
TOTAL							

SNACKS	
TIME	

	CORE BODY	UPPER BODY	LOWER BODY
EXERCISES			
SETS			
REPS			
WEIGHTS			
REST TIME			

	WARM UP	COOL DOWN
ACTIVITY		
SETS		
REPS		
TIME		
DIST		
INTENSITY		

GOALS: _____

_____

_____

_____

_____

_____

_____

_____

_____

DAY: _____

NAME: _____

	DESCRIPTION	QTY	PROTEINS	VEGGIES	FRUITS & NUTS	FATS
BREAKFAST						
TIME						
☐						
TOTAL						

LUNCH						
TIME						
☐						
TOTAL						

DINNER						
TIME						
☐						
TOTAL						

SNACKS	
TIME	
☐	

	CORE BODY	UPPER BODY	LOWER BODY
EXERCISES			
SETS			
REPS			
WEIGHTS			
REST TIME			

	WARM UP	COOL DOWN
ACTIVITY		
SETS		
REPS		
TIME		
DIST		
INTENSITY		

GOALS: _____

_____

_____

_____

_____

_____

_____

_____

DAY: _____

NAME: _____

		DESCRIPTION	QTY	PROTEINS	VEGGIES	FRUITS & NUTS	FATS
BREAKFAST							
TIME							
⬜							
TOTAL							

		DESCRIPTION	QTY	PROTEINS	VEGGIES	FRUITS & NUTS	FATS
LUNCH							
TIME							
⬜							
TOTAL							

		DESCRIPTION	QTY	PROTEINS	VEGGIES	FRUITS & NUTS	FATS
DINNER							
TIME							
⬜							
TOTAL							

SNACKS	
TIME	
⬜	

	CORE BODY	UPPER BODY	LOWER BODY
EXERCISES			
SETS			
REPS			
WEIGHTS			
REST TIME			

	WARM UP	COOL DOWN
ACTIVITY		
SETS		
REPS		
TIME		
DIST		
INTENSITY		

GOALS: _____

_____

_____

_____

_____

_____

_____

_____

_____

DAY: _____

NAME: _____

	DESCRIPTION	QTY	PROTEINS	VEGGIES	FRUITS & NUTS	FATS
BREAKFAST						
TIME						
TOTAL						

LUNCH						
TIME						
TOTAL						

DINNER						
TIME						
TOTAL						

SNACKS	
TIME	

	CORE BODY	UPPER BODY	LOWER BODY
EXERCISES			
SETS			
REPS			
WEIGHTS			
REST TIME			

	WARM UP	COOL DOWN
ACTIVITY		
SETS		
REPS		
TIME		
DIST		
INTENSITY		

GOALS: _____

_____

_____

_____

_____

_____

_____

_____

_____

DAY: _____

NAME: _____

		DESCRIPTION	QTY	PROTEINS	VEGGIES	FRUITS & NUTS	FATS
BREAKFAST							
TIME							
TOTAL							

LUNCH							
TIME							
TOTAL							

DINNER							
TIME							
TOTAL							

SNACKS		
TIME		

	CORE BODY	UPPER BODY	LOWER BODY
EXERCISES			
SETS			
REPS			
WEIGHTS			
REST TIME			

	WARM UP	COOL DOWN
ACTIVITY		
SETS		
REPS		
TIME		
DIST		
INTENSITY		

GOALS: _____

_____

_____

_____

_____

_____

_____

_____

DAY: _____

NAME: _____

	DESCRIPTION	QTY	PROTEINS	VEGGIES	FRUITS & NUTS	FATS
BREAKFAST						
TIME						
TOTAL						

LUNCH						
TIME						
TOTAL						

DINNER						
TIME						
TOTAL						

SNACKS	
TIME	

	CORE BODY	UPPER BODY	LOWER BODY
EXERCISES			
SETS			
REPS			
WEIGHTS			
REST TIME			

	WARM UP	COOL DOWN
ACTIVITY		
SETS		
REPS		
TIME		
DIST		
INTENSITY		

GOALS: _____

_____

_____

_____

_____

_____

_____

_____

_____

DAY: _____

NAME: _____

		DESCRIPTION	QTY	PROTEINS	VEGGIES	FRUITS & NUTS	FATS
BREAKFAST							
TIME							
TOTAL							

LUNCH						
TIME						
TOTAL						

DINNER						
TIME						
TOTAL						

SNACKS	
TIME	

	CORE BODY	UPPER BODY	LOWER BODY
EXERCISES			
SETS			
REPS			
WEIGHTS			
REST TIME			

	WARM UP	COOL DOWN
ACTIVITY		
SETS		
REPS		
TIME		
DIST		
INTENSITY		

GOALS: _____

_____

_____

_____

_____

_____

_____

_____

DAY: _____

NAME: _____

	DESCRIPTION	QTY	PROTEINS	VEGGIES	FRUITS & NUTS	FATS
BREAKFAST **TIME** [ ]						
TOTAL						

LUNCH **TIME** [ ]						
TOTAL						

DINNER **TIME** [ ]						
TOTAL						

SNACKS **TIME** [ ]	

	CORE BODY	UPPER BODY	LOWER BODY
EXERCISES			
SETS			
REPS			
WEIGHTS			
REST TIME			

	WARM UP	COOL DOWN
ACTIVITY		
SETS		
REPS		
TIME		
DIST		
INTENSITY		

GOALS: _____

_____

_____

_____

_____

_____

_____

_____

DAY: _____

NAME: _____

		DESCRIPTION	QTY	PROTEINS	VEGGIES	FRUITS & NUTS	FATS
BREAKFAST							
TIME							
TOTAL							

LUNCH							
TIME							
TOTAL							

DINNER							
TIME							
TOTAL							

SNACKS	
TIME	

	CORE BODY	UPPER BODY	LOWER BODY
EXERCISES			
SETS			
REPS			
WEIGHTS			
REST TIME			

	WARM UP	COOL DOWN
ACTIVITY		
SETS		
REPS		
TIME		
DIST		
INTENSITY		

GOALS: _____

_____

_____

_____

_____

_____

_____

_____

DAY: _____

NAME: _____

	DESCRIPTION	QTY	PROTEINS	VEGGIES	FRUITS & NUTS	FATS
BREAKFAST						
TIME						
TOTAL						

LUNCH						
TIME						
TOTAL						

DINNER						
TIME						
TOTAL						

SNACKS	
TIME	

	CORE BODY	UPPER BODY	LOWER BODY
EXERCISES			
SETS			
REPS			
WEIGHTS			
REST TIME			

	WARM UP	COOL DOWN
ACTIVITY		
SETS		
REPS		
TIME		
DIST		
INTENSITY		

GOALS: _____

_____

_____

_____

_____

_____

_____

_____

_____

DAY: _____

NAME: _____

		DESCRIPTION	QTY	PROTEINS	VEGGIES	FRUITS & NUTS	FATS
BREAKFAST							
TIME							
TOTAL							

LUNCH							
TIME							
TOTAL							

DINNER							
TIME							
TOTAL							

SNACKS	
TIME	

	CORE BODY	UPPER BODY	LOWER BODY
EXERCISES			
SETS			
REPS			
WEIGHTS			
REST TIME			

	WARM UP	COOL DOWN
ACTIVITY		
SETS		
REPS		
TIME		
DIST		
INTENSITY		

GOALS: _____

_____

_____

_____

_____

_____

_____

_____

_____

DAY: _____

NAME: _____

	DESCRIPTION	QTY	PROTEINS	VEGGIES	FRUITS & NUTS	FATS
BREAKFAST						
TIME						
TOTAL						

LUNCH						
TIME						
TOTAL						

DINNER						
TIME						
TOTAL						

SNACKS	
TIME	

	CORE BODY	UPPER BODY	LOWER BODY
EXERCISES			
SETS			
REPS			
WEIGHTS			
REST TIME			

	WARM UP	COOL DOWN
ACTIVITY		
SETS		
REPS		
TIME		
DIST		
INTENSITY		

GOALS: _____

_____

_____

_____

_____

_____

_____

_____

_____

DAY: _____

NAME: _____

		DESCRIPTION	QTY	PROTEINS	VEGGIES	FRUITS & NUTS	FATS
BREAKFAST							
TIME							
TOTAL							

LUNCH							
TIME							
TOTAL							

DINNER							
TIME							
TOTAL							

SNACKS	
TIME	

	CORE BODY	UPPER BODY	LOWER BODY
EXERCISES			
SETS			
REPS			
WEIGHTS			
REST TIME			

	WARM UP	COOL DOWN
ACTIVITY		
SETS		
REPS		
TIME		
DIST		
INTENSITY		

GOALS: _____

_____

_____

_____

_____

_____

_____

_____

_____

DAY: _____

NAME: _____

	DESCRIPTION	QTY	PROTEINS	VEGGIES	FRUITS & NUTS	FATS
BREAKFAST						
TIME						
TOTAL						

LUNCH						
TIME						
TOTAL						

DINNER						
TIME						
TOTAL						

SNACKS	
TIME	

	CORE BODY	UPPER BODY	LOWER BODY
EXERCISES			
SETS			
REPS			
WEIGHTS			
REST TIME			

	WARM UP	COOL DOWN
ACTIVITY		
SETS		
REPS		
TIME		
DIST		
INTENSITY		

GOALS: _____

_____

_____

_____

_____

_____

_____

_____

_____

DAY: _____

NAME: _____

	DESCRIPTION	QTY	PROTEINS	VEGGIES	FRUITS & NUTS	FATS
BREAKFAST						
TIME						
TOTAL						

LUNCH						
TIME						
TOTAL						

DINNER						
TIME						
TOTAL						

SNACKS	
TIME	

	CORE BODY	UPPER BODY	LOWER BODY
EXERCISES			
SETS			
REPS			
WEIGHTS			
REST TIME			

	WARM UP	COOL DOWN
ACTIVITY		
SETS		
REPS		
TIME		
DIST		
INTENSITY		

GOALS: _____

_____

_____

_____

_____

_____

_____

_____

_____

DAY: _____

NAME: _____

	DESCRIPTION	QTY	PROTEINS	VEGGIES	FRUITS & NUTS	FATS
BREAKFAST						
TIME						
TOTAL						

LUNCH						
TIME						
TOTAL						

DINNER						
TIME						
TOTAL						

SNACKS	
TIME	

	CORE BODY	UPPER BODY	LOWER BODY
EXERCISES			
SETS			
REPS			
WEIGHTS			
REST TIME			

	WARM UP	COOL DOWN
ACTIVITY		
SETS		
REPS		
TIME		
DIST		
INTENSITY		

GOALS: _____

_____

_____

_____

_____

_____

_____

_____

_____

DAY: _____

NAME: _____

	DESCRIPTION	QTY	PROTEINS	VEGGIES	FRUITS & NUTS	FATS
BREAKFAST						
TIME						
TOTAL						

LUNCH						
TIME						
TOTAL						

DINNER						
TIME						
TOTAL						

SNACKS	
TIME	

	CORE BODY	UPPER BODY	LOWER BODY
EXERCISES			
SETS			
REPS			
WEIGHTS			
REST TIME			

	WARM UP	COOL DOWN
ACTIVITY		
SETS		
REPS		
TIME		
DIST		
INTENSITY		

GOALS: _____

_____

_____

_____

_____

_____

_____

_____

_____

_____

DAY: _____

NAME: _____

	DESCRIPTION	QTY	PROTEINS	VEGGIES	FRUITS & NUTS	FATS
BREAKFAST **TIME** ☐						
TOTAL						

LUNCH **TIME** ☐						
TOTAL						

DINNER **TIME** ☐						
TOTAL						

SNACKS **TIME** ☐	

	CORE BODY	UPPER BODY	LOWER BODY
EXERCISES			
SETS			
REPS			
WEIGHTS			
REST TIME			

	WARM UP	COOL DOWN
ACTIVITY		
SETS		
REPS		
TIME		
DIST		
INTENSITY		

GOALS: _____

_____

_____

_____

_____

_____

_____

_____

_____

_____

DAY: _____

NAME: _____

	DESCRIPTION	QTY	PROTEINS	VEGGIES	FRUITS & NUTS	FATS
BREAKFAST						
TIME						
TOTAL						

LUNCH						
TIME						
TOTAL						

DINNER						
TIME						
TOTAL						

SNACKS	
TIME	

	CORE BODY	UPPER BODY	LOWER BODY
EXERCISES			
SETS			
REPS			
WEIGHTS			
REST TIME			

	WARM UP	COOL DOWN
ACTIVITY		
SETS		
REPS		
TIME		
DIST		
INTENSITY		

GOALS: _____

_____

_____

_____

_____

_____

_____

_____

_____

_____

DAY: _____

NAME: _____

	DESCRIPTION	QTY	PROTEINS	VEGGIES	FRUITS & NUTS	FATS
BREAKFAST **TIME**						
TOTAL						

LUNCH **TIME**						
TOTAL						

DINNER **TIME**						
TOTAL						

SNACKS **TIME**	

	CORE BODY	UPPER BODY	LOWER BODY
EXERCISES			
SETS			
REPS			
WEIGHTS			
REST TIME			

	WARM UP	COOL DOWN
ACTIVITY		
SETS		
REPS		
TIME		
DIST		
INTENSITY		

GOALS: _____

_____

_____

_____

_____

_____

_____

_____

_____

_____

DAY: _____

NAME: _____

	DESCRIPTION	QTY	PROTEINS	VEGGIES	FRUITS & NUTS	FATS
BREAKFAST						
TIME						
TOTAL						

LUNCH						
TIME						
TOTAL						

DINNER						
TIME						
TOTAL						

SNACKS	
TIME	

	CORE BODY	UPPER BODY	LOWER BODY
EXERCISES			
SETS			
REPS			
WEIGHTS			
REST TIME			

	WARM UP	COOL DOWN
ACTIVITY		
SETS		
REPS		
TIME		
DIST		
INTENSITY		

GOALS: _____

_____

_____

_____

_____

_____

_____

_____

_____

DAY: _____

NAME: _____

	DESCRIPTION	QTY	PROTEINS	VEGGIES	FRUITS & NUTS	FATS
BREAKFAST TIME ☐						
TOTAL						

LUNCH TIME ☐						
TOTAL						

DINNER TIME ☐						
TOTAL						

SNACKS TIME ☐	

	CORE BODY	UPPER BODY	LOWER BODY
EXERCISES			
SETS			
REPS			
WEIGHTS			
REST TIME			

	WARM UP	COOL DOWN
ACTIVITY		
SETS		
REPS		
TIME		
DIST		
INTENSITY		

GOALS: _____

_____

_____

_____

_____

_____

_____

_____

_____

DAY: _____

NAME: _____

		DESCRIPTION	QTY	PROTEINS	VEGGIES	FRUITS & NUTS	FATS
BREAKFAST							
TIME							
TOTAL							

		DESCRIPTION	QTY	PROTEINS	VEGGIES	FRUITS & NUTS	FATS
LUNCH							
TIME							
TOTAL							

		DESCRIPTION	QTY	PROTEINS	VEGGIES	FRUITS & NUTS	FATS
DINNER							
TIME							
TOTAL							

SNACKS	
TIME	

	CORE BODY	UPPER BODY	LOWER BODY
EXERCISES			
SETS			
REPS			
WEIGHTS			
REST TIME			

	WARM UP	COOL DOWN
ACTIVITY		
SETS		
REPS		
TIME		
DIST		
INTENSITY		

GOALS: _____

_____

_____

_____

_____

_____

_____

_____

_____

DAY: _____

NAME: _____

	DESCRIPTION	QTY	PROTEINS	VEGGIES	FRUITS & NUTS	FATS
BREAKFAST						
TIME						
TOTAL						

LUNCH						
TIME						
TOTAL						

DINNER						
TIME						
TOTAL						

SNACKS	
TIME	

	CORE BODY	UPPER BODY	LOWER BODY
EXERCISES			
SETS			
REPS			
WEIGHTS			
REST TIME			

	WARM UP	COOL DOWN
ACTIVITY		
SETS		
REPS		
TIME		
DIST		
INTENSITY		

GOALS: _____

_____

_____

_____

_____

_____

_____

_____

DAY: _____

NAME: _____

		DESCRIPTION	QTY	PROTEINS	VEGGIES	FRUITS & NUTS	FATS
BREAKFAST							
TIME							
TOTAL							

		DESCRIPTION	QTY	PROTEINS	VEGGIES	FRUITS & NUTS	FATS
LUNCH							
TIME							
TOTAL							

		DESCRIPTION	QTY	PROTEINS	VEGGIES	FRUITS & NUTS	FATS
DINNER							
TIME							
TOTAL							

SNACKS	
TIME	

	CORE BODY	UPPER BODY	LOWER BODY
EXERCISES			
SETS			
REPS			
WEIGHTS			
REST TIME			

	WARM UP	COOL DOWN
ACTIVITY		
SETS		
REPS		
TIME		
DIST		
INTENSITY		

GOALS: _____

_____

_____

_____

_____

_____

_____

_____

_____

DAY: _____

NAME: _____

	DESCRIPTION	QTY	PROTEINS	VEGGIES	FRUITS & NUTS	FATS
BREAKFAST						
TIME						
TOTAL						

LUNCH						
TIME						
TOTAL						

DINNER						
TIME						
TOTAL						

SNACKS	
TIME	

	CORE BODY	UPPER BODY	LOWER BODY
EXERCISES			
SETS			
REPS			
WEIGHTS			
REST TIME			

	WARM UP	COOL DOWN
ACTIVITY		
SETS		
REPS		
TIME		
DIST		
INTENSITY		

GOALS: _____

_____

_____

_____

_____

_____

_____

_____

_____

DAY: _____

NAME: _____

		DESCRIPTION	QTY	PROTEINS	VEGGIES	FRUITS & NUTS	FATS
BREAKFAST							
TIME							
☐							
TOTAL							

LUNCH							
TIME							
☐							
TOTAL							

DINNER							
TIME							
☐							
TOTAL							

SNACKS	
TIME	
☐	

	CORE BODY	UPPER BODY	LOWER BODY
EXERCISES			
SETS			
REPS			
WEIGHTS			
REST TIME			

	WARM UP	COOL DOWN
ACTIVITY		
SETS		
REPS		
TIME		
DIST		
INTENSITY		

GOALS: _____

_____

_____

_____

_____

_____

_____

_____

_____

DAY: _____

NAME: _____

	DESCRIPTION	QTY	PROTEINS	VEGGIES	FRUITS & NUTS	FATS
BREAKFAST TIME						
TOTAL						

LUNCH TIME						
TOTAL						

DINNER TIME						
TOTAL						

SNACKS TIME	

	CORE BODY	UPPER BODY	LOWER BODY
EXERCISES			
SETS			
REPS			
WEIGHTS			
REST TIME			

	WARM UP	COOL DOWN
ACTIVITY		
SETS		
REPS		
TIME		
DIST		
INTENSITY		

GOALS: _____

_____

_____

_____

_____

_____

_____

_____

_____

DAY: _____

NAME: _____

	DESCRIPTION	QTY	PROTEINS	VEGGIES	FRUITS & NUTS	FATS
BREAKFAST						
TIME ☐						
TOTAL						

LUNCH						
TIME ☐						
TOTAL						

DINNER						
TIME ☐						
TOTAL						

SNACKS	
TIME ☐	

	CORE BODY	UPPER BODY	LOWER BODY
EXERCISES			
SETS			
REPS			
WEIGHTS			
REST TIME			

	WARM UP	COOL DOWN
ACTIVITY		
SETS		
REPS		
TIME		
DIST		
INTENSITY		

GOALS: _____

_____

_____

_____

_____

_____

_____

_____

_____

DAY: _____

NAME: _____

	DESCRIPTION	QTY	PROTEINS	VEGGIES	FRUITS & NUTS	FATS
BREAKFAST						
TIME						
TOTAL						

LUNCH						
TIME						
TOTAL						

DINNER						
TIME						
TOTAL						

SNACKS	
TIME	

	CORE BODY	UPPER BODY	LOWER BODY
EXERCISES			
SETS			
REPS			
WEIGHTS			
REST TIME			

	WARM UP	COOL DOWN
ACTIVITY		
SETS		
REPS		
TIME		
DIST		
INTENSITY		

GOALS: _____

_____

_____

_____

_____

_____

_____

_____

DAY: _____

NAME: _____

		DESCRIPTION	QTY	PROTEINS	VEGGIES	FRUITS & NUTS	FATS
BREAKFAST							
TIME							
TOTAL							

LUNCH							
TIME							
TOTAL							

DINNER							
TIME							
TOTAL							

SNACKS	
TIME	

	CORE BODY	UPPER BODY	LOWER BODY
EXERCISES			
SETS			
REPS			
WEIGHTS			
REST TIME			

	WARM UP	COOL DOWN
ACTIVITY		
SETS		
REPS		
TIME		
DIST		
INTENSITY		

GOALS: _____

_____

_____

_____

_____

_____

_____

_____

_____

DAY: _____

NAME: _____

	DESCRIPTION	QTY	PROTEINS	VEGGIES	FRUITS & NUTS	FATS
BREAKFAST						
TIME						
TOTAL						

LUNCH						
TIME						
TOTAL						

DINNER						
TIME						
TOTAL						

SNACKS	
TIME	

	CORE BODY	UPPER BODY	LOWER BODY
EXERCISES			
SETS			
REPS			
WEIGHTS			
REST TIME			

	WARM UP	COOL DOWN
ACTIVITY		
SETS		
REPS		
TIME		
DIST		
INTENSITY		

GOALS: _____

_____

_____

_____

_____

_____

_____

_____

_____

DAY: _____

NAME: _____

	DESCRIPTION	QTY	PROTEINS	VEGGIES	FRUITS & NUTS	FATS
BREAKFAST						
TIME						
TOTAL						

LUNCH						
TIME						
TOTAL						

DINNER						
TIME						
TOTAL						

SNACKS	
TIME	

	CORE BODY	UPPER BODY	LOWER BODY
EXERCISES			
SETS			
REPS			
WEIGHTS			
REST TIME			

	WARM UP	COOL DOWN
ACTIVITY		
SETS		
REPS		
TIME		
DIST		
INTENSITY		

GOALS: _____

_____

_____

_____

_____

_____

_____

_____

_____

_____

DAY: _____

NAME: _____

	DESCRIPTION	QTY	PROTEINS	VEGGIES	FRUITS & NUTS	FATS
BREAKFAST						
TIME						
TOTAL						

LUNCH						
TIME						
TOTAL						

DINNER						
TIME						
TOTAL						

SNACKS	
TIME	

	CORE BODY	UPPER BODY	LOWER BODY
EXERCISES			
SETS			
REPS			
WEIGHTS			
REST TIME			

	WARM UP	COOL DOWN
ACTIVITY		
SETS		
REPS		
TIME		
DIST		
INTENSITY		

GOALS: _____

_____

_____

_____

_____

_____

_____

_____

_____

DAY: _____

NAME: _____

	DESCRIPTION	QTY	PROTEINS	VEGGIES	FRUITS & NUTS	FATS
BREAKFAST						
TIME						
TOTAL						

LUNCH						
TIME						
TOTAL						

DINNER						
TIME						
TOTAL						

SNACKS	
TIME	

	CORE BODY	UPPER BODY	LOWER BODY
EXERCISES			
SETS			
REPS			
WEIGHTS			
REST TIME			

	WARM UP	COOL DOWN
ACTIVITY		
SETS		
REPS		
TIME		
DIST		
INTENSITY		

GOALS: _____

_____

_____

_____

_____

_____

_____

_____

DAY: _____

NAME: _____

	DESCRIPTION	QTY	PROTEINS	VEGGIES	FRUITS & NUTS	FATS
BREAKFAST **TIME**						
TOTAL						

LUNCH **TIME**						
TOTAL						

DINNER **TIME**						
TOTAL						

SNACKS **TIME**	

	CORE BODY	UPPER BODY	LOWER BODY
EXERCISES			
SETS			
REPS			
WEIGHTS			
REST TIME			

	WARM UP	COOL DOWN
ACTIVITY		
SETS		
REPS		
TIME		
DIST		
INTENSITY		

GOALS: _____

_____

_____

_____

_____

_____

_____

_____

_____

DAY: _____

NAME: _____

	DESCRIPTION	QTY	PROTEINS	VEGGIES	FRUITS & NUTS	FATS
BREAKFAST						
TIME						
TOTAL						

LUNCH						
TIME						
TOTAL						

DINNER						
TIME						
TOTAL						

SNACKS	
TIME	

	CORE BODY	UPPER BODY	LOWER BODY
EXERCISES			
SETS			
REPS			
WEIGHTS			
REST TIME			

	WARM UP	COOL DOWN
ACTIVITY		
SETS		
REPS		
TIME		
DIST		
INTENSITY		

GOALS: _____

_____

_____

_____

_____

_____

_____

_____

_____

DAY: _____

NAME: _____

	DESCRIPTION	QTY	PROTEINS	VEGGIES	FRUITS & NUTS	FATS
BREAKFAST						
TIME						
TOTAL						

LUNCH						
TIME						
TOTAL						

DINNER						
TIME						
TOTAL						

SNACKS	
TIME	

	CORE BODY	UPPER BODY	LOWER BODY
EXERCISES			
SETS			
REPS			
WEIGHTS			
REST TIME			

	WARM UP	COOL DOWN
ACTIVITY		
SETS		
REPS		
TIME		
DIST		
INTENSITY		

GOALS: _____

_____

_____

_____

_____

_____

_____

_____

_____

_____

DAY: _____

NAME: _____

		DESCRIPTION	QTY	PROTEINS	VEGGIES	FRUITS & NUTS	FATS
BREAKFAST							
TIME							
TOTAL							

LUNCH							
TIME							
TOTAL							

DINNER							
TIME							
TOTAL							

SNACKS	
TIME	

	CORE BODY	UPPER BODY	LOWER BODY
EXERCISES			
SETS			
REPS			
WEIGHTS			
REST TIME			

	WARM UP	COOL DOWN
ACTIVITY		
SETS		
REPS		
TIME		
DIST		
INTENSITY		

GOALS: _____

_____

_____

_____

_____

_____

_____

_____

_____

_____

DAY: _____

NAME: _____

	DESCRIPTION	QTY	PROTEINS	VEGGIES	FRUITS & NUTS	FATS
BREAKFAST						
TIME						
TOTAL						

LUNCH						
TIME						
TOTAL						

DINNER						
TIME						
TOTAL						

SNACKS	
TIME	

	CORE BODY	UPPER BODY	LOWER BODY
EXERCISES			
SETS			
REPS			
WEIGHTS			
REST TIME			

	WARM UP	COOL DOWN
ACTIVITY		
SETS		
REPS		
TIME		
DIST		
INTENSITY		

GOALS: _____

_____

_____

_____

_____

_____

_____

_____

_____

DAY: _____

NAME: _____

	DESCRIPTION	QTY	PROTEINS	VEGGIES	FRUITS & NUTS	FATS
BREAKFAST						
TIME						
TOTAL						

LUNCH						
TIME						
TOTAL						

DINNER						
TIME						
TOTAL						

SNACKS	
TIME	

	CORE BODY	UPPER BODY	LOWER BODY
EXERCISES			
SETS			
REPS			
WEIGHTS			
REST TIME			

	WARM UP	COOL DOWN
ACTIVITY		
SETS		
REPS		
TIME		
DIST		
INTENSITY		

GOALS: _____

_____

_____

_____

_____

_____

_____

_____

_____

www.ingramcontent.com/pod-product-compliance
Lightning Source LLC
Chambersburg PA
CBHW080739250626
47170CB00010B/2884